Professional Post-graduate Diploma in Marketing

Paper 10: Strategic Marketing Decisions

CW00515882

First edition October 2004

ISBN 0 7517 1757 6

British Library Cataloguing-in-Publication Data

A catalogue record for this book is available from the British Library

Published by

BPP Professional Education, Aldine House, Aldine Place, London W12 8AW

www.bpp.com

Printed in Great Britain by Ashford Colour Press

©

BPP Professional Education

2004

Welcome to BPP's CIM **Passcards**.

- They **save you time**. Important topics are summarised for you.

- They incorporate **diagrams** to kick start your memory.

- They follow the overall **structure** of the BPP Study Texts, but BPP's CIM **Passcards** are not just a condensed book. Each card has been separately designed for clear presentation. Topics are self contained and can be grasped visually.

- CIM **Passcards** are **just the right size** for pockets, briefcases and bags.

- CIM **Passcards focus on the exam**. They are also ideal **summaries** to aid you if you are taking the **assignment route**.

If you are taking the exam, run through the complete set of **Passcards** as often as you can during your final revision period. The day before the exam, try to go through the **Passcards** again! You will then be well on your way to passing. **Good luck!**

BPP also publishes a Practice and Revision Kit which contains a bank of questions for you to attempt during your final revision period.

Contents

Preface

1: The strategic background

This introductory chapter discusses material that forms a background to strategic management. The unifying theme is dealing with change in a variety of forms.

Topic List

The background to strategic decisions

The product life cycle

Experience, PIMS and market share

Marketing projects

Strategic decisions to sustain competitive advantage are made in a context of CHANGE.

Two important influences

- **Globalisation** brings new and larger markets and cost advantages. Strategists think globally, act locally.
- **The Internet:** routine purchasing requires little human involvement; information can be provided; web software and hardware create a new industry – but **fulfilment** is still demanding.

Examples of environmental change

- **Technology:** developments lead to new products and new methods.
- **Demographics:** in the EU the population is ageing. Migration will produce other effects.
- **Economic growth:** once stagnant economies such as China and India are growing rapidly.
- Large organisations are concentrating on design, marketing and service, **outsourcing** production to low-wage economies.

Product life cycle

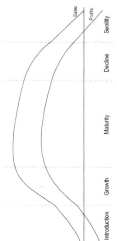

| Introduction | Growth | Maturity | Decline | Senility |

Introduction: development, marketing and production costs high; sales volume low; profits low

Growth: sales volumes accelerate, must costs fall, profits rise; competitors enter the market

Maturity: longest period; profits good; reminder promotion

Decline: many causes; sales fall, over capacity in industry; some players leave market

Senility: profit negligible; product may be retained in niche market

Using the PLC

■ Shape and duration vary between products and between product class, product form and brand.

■ *Ansoff* suggests a **demand life cycle** is made up of technology life cycles which are made up of plcs.

■ **Penetration** pricing speeds introduction and growth; **skimming** slows them down.

■ Market penetration also depends on:

– Network externalities, eg camera phones – who else has one?

– Existence of a common standard, eg DVD

– Existence of complementary products, eg computer games need computers

– Cost of experimentation

High output and high market share can lead to lower costs and higher profits.

Economies of scale

As output increases, cost per unit falls:

- Fixed costs are spread over more units
- Bulk purchasing of raw materials is possible
- Larger and more specialised machinery is used

The **experience effect** makes production more efficient as time goes by because of **learning** and product improvements.

PIMS

Profit impact of Marketing Strategies research shows a correlation between **market share** and **profit**. This is probably caused by economies of scale.

The correlation does not always hold good:

- Some industries have both small and large firms in profit but few profitable medium-sized ones
- A **niche** or focus strategy can be highly profitable.

A project 'has a beginning and an end and ... cost, schedule and quality objectives'. *(Haynes)*

Projects are common in marketing management at all levels.

The role of the project manager

- Outline and detailed planning
- Team building
- Communication: team and sponsors
- Co-ordinate project activities
- Monitor and control progress within costs, time and quality constraints
- Resolve problems

The project life cycle – 4Ds *(Maylor)*

- **Define** the project: identify what has to be done to meet specified needs
- **Design** the project: plan how the needs will be met and show benefits
- **Deliver** the project: assemble resources, carry out plan, deliver output
- **Develop** the process: review outcomes, document lessons for future use

2: Models of strategic management

This chapter extends the background to strategic decision-making by reviewing the ways in which organisations can approach strategy. The rational model is out of fashion as cumbersome, but it covers all the important points. The other models in this chapter tend to concentrate on more specific elements of the strategic process.

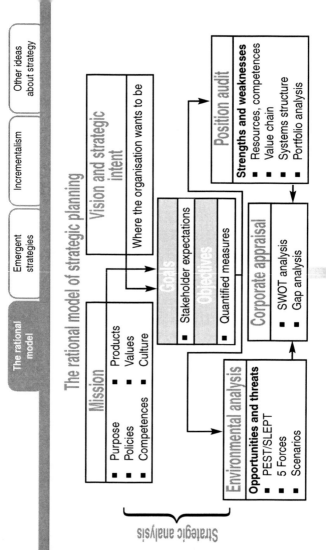

The rational model of strategic planning

Other ideas about strategy	Incrementalism	Emergent strategies	The rational model

Mission
- Purpose
- Policies
- Competences
- Products
- Values
- Culture

Vision and strategic intent

Where the organisation wants to be

Goals
- Stakeholder expectations

Objectives
- Quantified measures

Environmental analysis

Opportunities and threats
- PEST/SLEPT
- 5 Forces
- Scenarios

Position audit

Strengths and weaknesses
- Resources, competences
- Value chain
- Systems structure
- Portfolio analysis

Corporate appraisal
- SWOT analysis
- Gap analysis

Strategic analysis

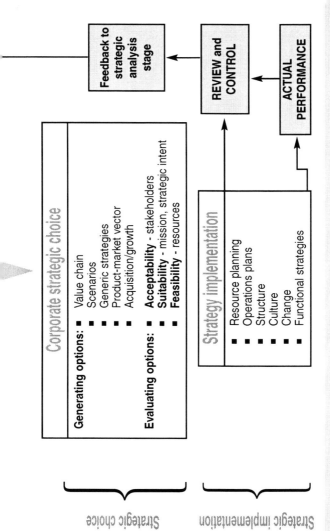

Corporate strategic choice

Generating options:
- Value chain
- Scenarios
- Generic strategies
- Product-market vector
- Acquisition/growth

Evaluating options:
- **Acceptability** - stakeholders
- **Suitability** - mission, strategic intent
- **Feasibility** - resources

Strategy implementation
- Resource planning
- Operations plans
- Structure
- Culture
- Change
- Functional strategies

Feedback to strategic analysis stage

REVIEW and CONTROL

ACTUAL PERFORMANCE

Strategic choice

Strategic implementation

2: Models of strategic management

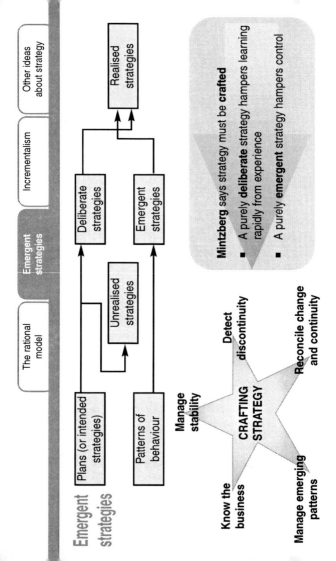

The rational model | Emergent strategies | Incrementalism | Other ideas about strategy

Emergent strategies

Plans (or intended strategies) → Deliberate strategies → Realised strategies

Plans (or intended strategies) → Unrealised strategies

Patterns of behaviour → Emergent strategies → Realised strategies

Mintzberg says strategy must be **crafted**

- A purely **deliberate** strategy hampers learning rapidly from experience
- A purely **emergent** strategy hampers control

CRAFTING STRATEGY

- Detect discontinuity
- Reconcile change and continuity
- Manage emerging patterns
- Know the business
- Manage stability

Bounded rationality

Strategic managers' decision making is constrained by the time and amount of information available to them and by their own skills, habits and awareness.

They:

- Do **not** consider all options, but choose from a restricted range

- Make political compromises by **partisan mutual adjustment**

- **Satisfice** rather than optimise

Incrementalism

Development by small scale extensions of past practices.

This approach avoids major errors by the exercise of caution and produces acceptable solutions because it uses consultation, compromise and accommodation.

Logical incrementalism combines this approach with an in-depth review to establish the broad outlines of strategy.

Management action

Andrews suggests strategy arises from the pattern of decisions that make up the general management process. *Johnson and Scholes* recognise the importance of an acknowledged person or group in overall change. They also identify the **paradigm** (collectively held assumptions and beliefs) and **politics** (bargaining and negotiation between interest groups) as important.

Entrepreneurial individuals may succeed by means of **free wheeling opportunism**.

Internal or external focus?

Strategy may be built on **distinctive** (or core) **competences** within the organisation including **knowledge**.

Strategy may be based on seeking **environmental fit**, possibly by moulding the firm, possibly by creating the future and moulding the environment.

Common sense would suggest these are not really alternatives and a successful strategy will involve both approaches.

Notes

3: Planning for the future

This chapter draws together a number of topics that are all related to managing and planning future performance. These topics cover a range of disparate thinking, but each has potential for application in connection with decisions affecting the organisation's future progress.

Topic List

Innovations

Gap analysis

Forecasting

Scenario planning

Knowledge management

Small organisations

| Innovations |

Innovations

Businesses must innovate in order to respond to environmental changes, particularly social and technological ones. Innovation can affect both products and methods.

Innovation requires delegation, imagination, experiment and hard work. The managerial problem is to respond to a rapidly changing environment without losing control. *Burns and Stalker* identified a spectrum of innovatory capacity and ability to deal with a dynamic environment whose extremes were the **mechanistic** and **organismic** (or organic) organisations.

Mechanistic

Essentially, bureaucracies, these organisations use methodical procedures to promote efficiency. Work is standardised and control is effective. However, response to environmental change can be slow and faltering. The overall mission may be hampered by excess attention to detail and respect for procedure and precedent.

Organismic (or organic)

The common task is well understood and kept in view. Relationships are informal and fluid; hierarchy does not hamper action. There is frequent consultative and advisory communication. Control is cultural rather than procedural. The organisation is responsive and nimble.

Gap analysis

Gap analysis compares the sum of current projections with overall objectives and identifies means by which any gap between the two might be filled.

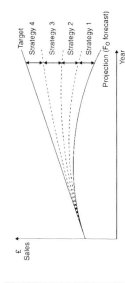

A forecast is made based on current plans for sales, costs and profits. This must also allow for environmental factors and be as accurate as possible.

Options for filling the gap are considered. The eventual plan may involve several projects addressing sales, revenues, costs and methods.

This is a type of **feedforward** control.

3: Planning for the future

Forecasting

Statistical forecasts assume that the past is a good guide to the future

- **Time series** analysis separates cyclical fluctuations from the underlying long term **trend**.

- **Regression analysis** measures the **correlation** between two **variables**.

- **Leading indicators**, change before the bulk of economic activity

Judgemental forecasts can be accurate or inaccurate. They are guesses based on education and experience.

Models are simplified representations of reality. Predictive models include the product life cycle and cost-volume-profit analysis.

The **Delphi method** polls experts separately for their opinions. Variations of opinion are re-examined anonymously to see if a consensus will emerge.

Market forecasts assess environmental factors outside the organisation's control.

Sales forecasts cover a shorter period and assess both uncontrollable and controllable factors (the marketing mix) affecting demand for a particular product.

Scenario planning

Scenario planning builds a number of different, comprehensive views of the future.

Steps in scenario planning

1. Identify drivers of change – major issues – 10 year horizon

2. Combine drivers in a framework – patterns, trends, intuition

3. Produce 7–9 mini scenarios

4. Group into 2–3 longer scenarios
   – highlights fundamental issues
   – scenarios are complementary, not competitive

5. Write the scenarios

6. Identify issues arising – critical outcomes, branching points, implications for key players

An industry scenario is an internally consistent view of an industry's future development

Using scenarios

Basing strategy on one scenario only is risky, while covering all possibilities is expensive.

There are several approaches.

- **The most probable** – insufficient coverage
- **Hope for the best** – too risky
- **Hedge** – sub optimal but safe
- **Influence the future** – risky but can bring great rewards

Knowledge management

Knowledge can be a major source of competitive advantage. The aim of knowledge management is to exploit existing knowledge and create new knowledge so that it may be exploited in turn.

	Data	Information	Knowledge
Nature	Facts	Relationships between processed facts	Patterns discerned in information
Importance of context	Total	Some	Context independent
Importance to business	Mundane	Probably useful for management	May be strategically useful
Relevant IT systems	Office automation Data warehouse	Groupware Expert systems Report writing software Intranet	Datamining Intranet Expert systems

> A **data warehouse** receives data from operational systems (eg sales order processing) and stores it without summarisation. **Data mining** software may then be able to discover the previously unobserved patterns and relationships that constitute strategically useful **knowledge**.

Small organisations have their own strategic problems, as do business start-ups

Small organisations

- Lack of economies of scale
- Burden of regulation and compliance
- Dependence on key individuals
- Restricted markets and product range
- Difficulty in raising capital
- Limited strategic experience or awareness

Start-ups

- Early losses and drain on **capital**
- Poor **cashflow** and cash management
- Lack of a wide range of **management skills**, especially in marketing and HRM
- The effect of the **business cycle**: a business that does reasonably well on the upswing but not wonderfully may fail when times are hard

Notes

4: Strategic advantage

While it is not always possible to obtain a significant advantage over competitors, survival and prosperity demand that businesses should strive to do so. Strategic competitive advantage can be pursued by a wide range of methods. This chapter deals with those methods, but commences with a discussion of how likely routes to success can be identified.

| Shareholder value analysis | Competitive strategy | Sustainable competitive advantage | Competitive positions |

The creation of value for shareholders by appropriate investment decisions is widely accepted as the proper objective of business activity.

Economic profit

Theory suggests computing shareholder value in terms of **economic profit**, which is net operating profit after tax, less a charge for the use of capital. Assessment of investments for the future is easier if done in terms of forecast cashflows using **discounting** to compute **net present value.**

(See the Annex to this chapter.)

Value based management†

Management success is measured by the value they create for shareholders. This is as applicable to marketing managers as to any others. Purely marketing objectives are no longer acceptable as measures of success. Marketing managers must be prepared to demonstrate that their spending creates positive cashflows and valuable assets.

Cost leadership

Aims to be the lowest cost producer in the industry as a whole

Aspects of cost leadership

Economies of scale

Use of the newest production technology

Learning curve effect

Productivity improvement

Minimisation of overheads

Favourable access to inputs

Focus

Differentiation

Aims to exploit a product perceived as unique within the industry as a whole

Aspects of differentiation

Breakthrough products – radical performance advantage

Improved products – more cost-effective

Competitive products – unique combinations of features

- Brand image
- Special features
- Unique combination of **value activities**

Activity is restricted to a particular **segment** of the market. Either a cost leadership or differentiation strategy is then pursued. Such concentrated effort can be more effective, but the segment may be attacked by a larger firm.

4: Strategic advantage

Generic strategies and the five competitive forces

Competitive force	Advantages		Disadvantages	
	Cost leadership	Differentiation	Cost leadership	Differentiation
New entrants	Economies of scale raise entry barriers	Brand loyalty and perceived uniqueness are entry barriers		
Substitutes	Firm is not so vulnerable as its less cost-effective competitors to the threat of substitutes	Customer loyalty is a weapon against substitutes		
Customers	Customers cannot drive down prices further than the next most efficient competitor	Customers have no comparable alternative Brand loyalty should lower price sensitivity		Customers may no longer need the differentiating factor Sooner or later, customers become price sensitive
Suppliers	Flexibility to deal with cost increases	Higher margins can offset vulnerability to supplier price rises	Increase in input costs can reduce price advantages	
Industry rivalry	Firm remains profitable when rivals go under through excessive price competition	Unique features reduce direct competition	Technological change will require capital investment, or make production cheaper for competitors Competitors learn via imitation Cost concerns ignore product design or marketing issues	Imitation narrows differentiation

Sustainable competitive advantage

Competitive advantage exists in the customer's mind and is easily lost. **Strategic wear-out** occurs when established strategies are made irrelevant by market changes, competitor innovations and internal failures of management such as an inconsistent investment policy. Continuing review of both environmental and internal factors is needed to avoid this.

Competitive advantage	Example/comment
Better product in some way	Renault – safest car in its class
Perceived advantage or psychic benefit	Exclusivity (eg Harrods)
Global skills	BA
Low costs, **via high productivity or focus**	Discount retailers or supermarkets such as Lidl or Aldi
Better competences	Some firms are better at marketing or aligning technologies to markets than others
Superior assets	Property, cash or brands
Economies of scale	Size can be a source of competitive advantage
Attitude	This is partly related to culture and management abilities
Superior **relationships**	Companies can exploit business alliances and develop personal relationships

4: Strategic advantage

Competitive positions

Marketing strategies can be based on competitors rather than customers.

Attack strategies

- **Frontal.** Same marketing mix head on: risky since attacks strengths not weaknesses

- **Flanking.** Enter product markets where competitor is weak, to prepare for frontal attack

- **Encirclement.** Launch products into all segments and channels to dilute ability to retaliate

- **By pass.** Avoid confrontation by launching new products and entering new markets

- **Guerrilla.** Destabilise by small, unrelated attacks including harassment by law suits and poaching staff

Defence strategies

- **Position.** Consolidate resources in current product markets: offers a sitting target

- **Mobile.** Product development, market development and diversification avoid head-on battle

- **Pre-emptive.** Enter a segment in force before the competitor does so

- **Flank.** Occupy a position of potential future importance

- **Counter offensive.** Immediate response to competitor initiatives, eg by price outs

- **Strategic withdrawal.** can release resources for better use elsewhere

Different strategies are appropriate to different market positions.

Pioneers

Use any of the defence strategies

Challengers

Use any of the attack strategies

Followers

- **Cloners** follow closely, initiating aspects of the leader's marketing mix (**counterfeiters** make fakes)

- **Initiators** follow at a distance by introducing some differentiation

- **Adopters** modify and improve the leader's products. They may challenge the leader

Nichers

Nichers use a **focus** strategy, relying partly on segmentation and partly on specialisation of one of the types below:

- Geographic
- Quality/price
- Specific customer – a few customers
- End-user – one type of customer
- Vertical level – one point in the production/ distribution chain
- Product or service
- Channel

Product market strategies

Ansoff described the four possible growth vectors in the four cells in the diagram below: the **growth vector matrix**. Numbers in circles show relative riskiness.

Product

	Existing	New
Existing	① **Market penetration** ■ Maintain or increase market share ■ Dominate growth markets ■ Drive out competition from mature markets ■ Increase usage by existing customers	④ **Product development** ■ Launch new products ■ May require new competences ■ Forces competitors to follow suit ■ Discourages newcomers ■ Expensive
New	② **Market development** ■ New markets for current products ■ New geographic areas - export ■ New package sizes ■ New distribution channels ■ Differential pricing to suit new segments	⑯ **Diversification** Related Unrelated (conglomerate) Vertical Horizontal Forward Backward New **competences** will be required

Market

Horizontal integration

Development into activities that are competitive with or complementary to present activities; eg, electricity companies selling gas. Offers economies of scale.

Conglomerate diversification

- Spreads risk
- May obtain synergy (eg acquiring tax losses and brands, utilising distribution channels, pooling R+D.)

However:

- Unfamiliarity with new segments increases risk
- Downturn in one sector drags down the rest
- Cultural and management integration mismatches

Vertical integration

The organisation becomes its own supplier (backward vertical integration) or distributor (forward vertical integration).

- Secures supplies
- Stronger relationship with end-users
- Profits from all parts of value system
- Creates barriers to entry

However:

- 'More eggs in same end-market basket' (Ansoff) – more vulnerable to a single market
- Does not offer significant economies of scale

Other strategies

- Withdrawal (but NB exit barriers)
- Demerger
- Disposal of subsidiary

Organic growth

The development of internal resources
- Supports **learning** and is supported by it
- Consistent culture and management style
- Provides economies of scale
- Ease of control

However:
- Can be slow
- Not good for dealing with barriers to entry

Co-operative methods

Include consortia, joint ventures, licensing, franchising and sub-contracting. These methods can enhance access to resources of all kinds, achieve economies of scale, achieve synergy, enhance competences and reduce overheads without any sacrifice of autonomy.

Mergers and acquisitions

- Can overcome barriers to entry
- Can spread risk
- Can defend against predators
- Provides access to a variety of resources: products; managers; suppliers; production facilities; technology and skills; distribution facilities; cash; tax losses

However, many acquisitions fail to enhance shareholder value.
- Cost: the price is often too high
- Cultural problems, especially in management
- Top management egos can warp judgement
- Professional advisers drive the market
- Customers may be disturbed by changes

Declining markets

Markets decline because of changes in **customer needs** and the emergence of **alternative satisfactions,** including those based on **new technology.** Firms can survive in three ways.

- Revitalise the market by identifying new segments; introducing new products and new applications for old products; or by changing the nature of the market

- Become a profitable survivor by forcing, easing or buying out competitors

- Harvest and withdraw: reduce resources committed, take a short-term view of profits, do enough to retain customers and staff while profitable

Hostile markets

Hostile markets arise from over capacity, leading to predatory pricing and product proliferation. Cost-cutting weakens firms, leading to shakeout.

Firms survive by:

- Focus on large customers giving economies of scale

- Differentiation on intangibles like service in order to avoid commoditisation

- Offering a broad but controlled range of products

- Controlling costs without prejudicing future effectiveness

4: Strategic advantage

Compounding calculates the future value of an investment, at a given rate of interest, if the interest earned is re-invested each year.

£X-invested for n years at r% gives us £S in n years' time

and £S = £X $(1 + r)^n$.

In the example, £14,641 = £10,000 × £10,000 × 1.1^4. ➔

Discounting is the reverse process. It enables us to find the present value of an expected future cashflow. So, in our example, the £14,041 we expect in four year's time has a present value of £10,000 if discounted at 10%. We can re-arrange the compunding formula to find £X (the present value) from £S (the future value) : £X = £S × $\frac{1}{(1+r)^n}$.

The expression $\frac{1}{(1+r)^n}$ is called the discount factor. Discount factors for various values of n and r are tabulated in many publications.

Example: invest £10,000 for four years at 10% pa

Time	Sum	Interest	Total
0	10,000	–	10,000
1	10,000	1,000	11,000
2	11,000	1,100	12,100
3	12,100	1,210	13,310
4	13,310	1,331	14,641

Investment appraisal. Discounting cashflows is a very useful way to assess the value of investment proposals. So long as the likely cashflows can be estimated and a sensible discount rate is used, we can say whether a project is worth undertaking.

Example: Watkins plc needs to earn 15% on investments in order to pay its overheads and satisfy its shareholders. It is considering a project costing £5,000 that will pay £3,000 in the first year and £4,000 in the second. Is the project worth while?

We use discounting to calculate a **net present value.**

Time	Cashflow £	Discount factors at 15%	Present value £
0	(5,000)	1.000	(5,000)
1	3,000	$\frac{1}{(1.15)^1} = 0.870$	2,610
2	4,000	$\frac{1}{(1.15)^2} = 0.756$	3,024
		Net present value	+634

Notes

1 Negatives are shown in brackets and represent out flows.

2 The discount factor at time zero for any value of n or r is 1.

3 Cash flows during a period are assumed to take place at its end.

The positive NPV of £634 represents the value created by the investment. A negative NPV project **destroys value**.

This technique can be used to choose between competing projects: we choose the highest NPV.

Perpetuity

A special case – a perpetuity (P) is a constant income each year indefinitely into the future. The present value of a perpetuity is easily found:

$$PV = \frac{P}{r}$$

Thus we may see how much it is worth investing to obtain the perpetuity

Two general truths

- The further into the future a cashflow occurs, the lower its NPV for any given discount rate.

- The higher the discount rate used, the lower the NPV for any given future cashflow.

5: Competitive positions

We start this chapter with a discussion of the ways in which strategic options may be evaluated. The three criteria of suitability, acceptability and feasibility should be kept in mind throughout any consideration of possible strategic options. We go on to consider the related topics of segmentation, targeting and positioning and conclude the chapter with a consideration of the important subject of electronic commerce.

life cycle/portfolio matrix
STAGES OF INDUSTRY MATURITY

COMPETITIVE POSITION	Embryonic	Growth	Mature	Ageing
Dominant	Fast grow Start up	Fast grow Attain cost leadership Renew Defend position	Defend position Attain cost leadership Renew Fast grow	Defend position Focus Renew Grow with industry
Strong	Start up Differentiate Fast grow	Fast grow Catch up Attain cost leadership Differentiate	Attain cost leadership Renew, focus Differentiate Grow with industry	Find niche Hold niche Hang in Grow with industry Harvest
Favourable	Start up Differentiate Focus Fast grow	Differentiate, focus Catch up Grow with industry	Harvest, hang in Find niche, hold niche Renew, turnaround Differentiate, focus Grow with industry	Retrench Turnaround
Tenable	Start up Grow with industry Focus	Harvest, catch up Hold niche, hang in Find niche Turnaround Focus Grow with industry	Harvest Turnaround Find niche Retrench	Divest Retrench
Weak	Find niche Catch up Grow with industry	Turnaround Retrench	Withdraw Divest	Withdraw

Strategies should be assessed for **suitability, feasibility and acceptability**

Suitability is a question of **strategic logic**. A strategy should be suited to the firm's circumstances.

- Exploit strengths
- Rectify weaknesses
- Satisfy goals
- Fill performance gaps
- Neutralise threats
- Seize opportunities
- Suit culture
- Acceptable risk

Business profile analysis

Forecast strategic outcomes are scored against empirically determined PIMS success parameters to assess the likely value of a given strategy

Strategy screening

Choices are assisted by ranking, decision trees and scenario planning

Acceptability depends on the views of **stakeholders** and the influence they wield.

Stakeholder group	Interest
Internal Managers, employees	Jobs, benefits satisfaction
Connected Shareholders	Shareholder value in **financial terms**
External Banks Suppliers Customers Government The public	Financial performance Stable relationship Price, delivery Tax, employment Governance, environment

Mintzberg describes two **coalitions** that wield power

Internal
Strategic apex (CEO and board),
Managers, staff, culture

External
Owners, business associates,
unions, professional bodies, public

Each group has three options

Exit	Loyalty
	Voice

Feasibility depends on the availability of **resources**, particularly **finance** and **competences**. The acquisition of either may form a fundamental aspect of a chosen strategy.

Stakeholders' interests are likely to conflict. *Mendelow's* **stakeholder mapping** helps the organisation to establish its priorities and set up its system of corporate governance.

Strategy selection

- Choices may be constrained by outside influences
- **Risk** should be assessed
- **Strategic draft** must be avoided if an incremental or emergent approach is used

Ranking and scoring

Possible courses of action may be ranked by assessing them against objective criteria such as ROI, growth, effect on markets, competitive response. The importance of the criteria as well as the suitability of each course is reflected in the scores.

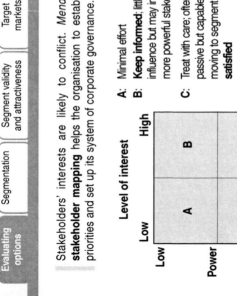

Level of interest

	Low	High
Low	A	B
High	C	D

Power

- **A:** Minimal effort
- **B:** **Keep informed**; little direct influence but may influence more powerful stakeholders
- **C:** Treat with care; often passive but capable of moving to segment D; **keep satisfied**
- **D:** **Key players** – strategy must be **acceptable** to them, at least

Markets are segmented so that groups of customers with similar needs and wants may be targeted with appropriately marketing mixes.

Steps in segmentation (Kotler)

1 Identify segmentation variables and segment the market

2 Develop segment profiles

3 Evaluate the attractiveness of each segment

4 Select the target segment(s)

5 Identify positioning concepts for each target segment

6 Select, develop and communicate the chosen concept

Industrial market segmentation bases

■ Location
■ Type and size of business
■ Use of product

Consumer market segmentation bases

■ Geographic
■ Demographic
  – Geodemographic, eg ACORN
  – Family life cycle
■ Psychographic (or lifestyle) – dimensions: activities, interests, opinions, demographics
■ Social class
  – UKONS classes 1–7 (from 2001)
  – JICNAR A, B, C1, C2, D, E
■ Behavioural – dimensions: product use, benefits expected attitude to risk, extent of use

Validity

A segment is only valid if it is worth designing a marketing mix to suit it. To be valid, a segment must be:

1. **Identifiable**
2. **Big enough**
3. **Stable**
4. **Reachable – profitably**

Attractiveness

Factors	Characteristics to examine
Market factors	<ul><li>Size of the segment</li><li>Segment growth rate</li><li>Stage of industry evaluation</li><li>Predictability</li><li>Price elasticity and sensitivity</li><li>Bargaining power of customers</li><li>Seasonality of demand</li></ul>
Economic and technological factors	<ul><li>Barriers to entry</li><li>Barriers to exit</li><li>Bargaining power of suppliers</li><li>Level of technology</li><li>Investment required</li><li>Margins available</li></ul>
Competitive factors	<ul><li>Competitive intensity</li><li>Quality of competition</li><li>Threat of substitution</li><li>Degree of differentiation</li></ul>
Environmental factors	<ul><li>Exposure to economic fluctuations</li><li>Exposure to political and legal factors</li><li>Degree of regulation</li><li>Social acceptability</li></ul>

Micromarketing

Where production technology can achieve **mass customisation** (a very wide range of available product persons and options on an almost bespoke basis), micromarketing is possible.

Micromarketing supports the growing range of **minority lifestyles** and exploits the fragmentation of the media to use highly targeted promotional activities.

Target market strategies

- **Undifferentiated marketing** or mass marketing ignores segmentation and works when the market is **homogeneous**.

- **Differentiated marketing** targets each valid segment with a different product. **Over-differentiation** occurs when the extra costs exceed the extra revenue. This can easily happen in the early stages of the product life cycle, when the total market is small.

- **Concentrated marketing** targets a single segment with a carefully specified product.

Positioning aims to achieve a distinctive and valued place for the market offering in the customer's mind.

Steps in positioning

1 Identify differentiating factors in products in relation to competitors.

2 Select the most important and easily communicated differences.

3 Communicate the position to the target market.

Positioning variable	Comment
Attributes	Size, for example
Benefit	What benefits we offer
Use/application	Ease of use; accessibility
User	The sort of person the product appeals to
Product category	Consciously differentiated from competition
Quality/price	One should support and validate the other, so that it makes sense to the customer and he understands what he is buying.

Mistake	Consequence
Underpositioning	The brand does not have a clear identity in the eyes of the customer
Overpositioning	Buyers may have too narrow an image of a brand
Confused positioning	Too many claims might be made for a brand
Doubtful positioning	The positioning may not be credible in the eyes of the buyer

Electronic data interchange (EDI)

EDI is an established method of linking industrial customers with their suppliers. The firm's computers are connected via a communications link and routine ordering and invoicing are done electronically. Paper records are reduced, clerical effort is saved and lead times are cut. However, there may be problems of system compatibility, time zone difference and the number of links that have to be managed and maintained.

Using the Internet

The Internet is about **information**, which is central to much marketing activity.

- **Marketing intelligence** is acquired when people register with Internet sites, particularly those used for selling.

- **Promotional information**, including advertising and public relations campaigns can be distributed via e-mail, websites, portals and search engines.

- Products and services that can be digitised such as music and newspapers can be distributed directly via the Internet, as can services such as banking, travel bookings and customer service.

- Physical products can be sold direct, though physical **fulfilment** is required.

Virtual companies

Electronic linking of geographically dispersed organisational elements can produce a **virtual organisation**. IT will be central to the production process; the company will have a flexible structure and a collaborative culture.

The impact of e-commerce

- Challenges traditional business models
- High visibility for small or specialist firms
- Extensive free information
- High speed communication for selling, purchasing and some distribution
- New intermediaries appear, older ones may disappear
- New business groups and partnerships
- Transparency of pricing via on-line comparisons
- New bases and methods of segmentation
- Dynamic pricing to reflect changing level of demand

Problems with e-commerce

- Links to existing business systems
- Threat to privacy
- Security of payment
- Fulfilment

A strategy for e-commerce

1 **Upgrade customer interaction:** automate response to FAQs; respond at least as fast as competitors; use e-mail; improve website.

2 **Understand customer segments:** identify those who will and will not ingrate to the website; attempt to automate service to low value customers; personalise for key customers.

3 **Understand service processes:** identify what can and cannot be automated and what customers will and will not accept.

4 **Define the role of live interaction:** useful for cross-selling; building trust; fast service and for some customers.

5 **Make the key technology decisions** about scale, pace and finance.

6 **Be prepared** for massive customer website usage: make the system user friendly, design it to be scaleable and provide as much capacity as possible.

7 **Create incentives** to use the e-commerce option: consider disincentives to personal interaction.

8 **Choose channels:** Physical, phone, post, Internet; and how they will interface with the relationship management database.

9 **Exploit Internet potential:** special sites for key accounts; proactive offerings; facilitate communities of users for referrals and product ideas; engage the buyer emotionally; promote repeat sales and turn browsers into buyers.

10 **Implement the chosen strategy**

6: Market entry methods

There is a large variety of methods that maybe used to enter a foreign market. Each has its own mix of risk, control, cost, benefits and drawbacks.

Topic List

Entry strategies

Strategic considerations

Exporting

Overseas production

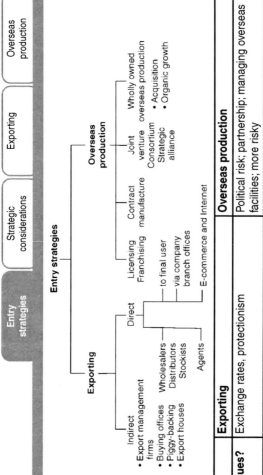

Entry strategies | Strategic considerations | Exporting | Overseas production

Entry strategies

- Exporting
  - Indirect
    - Export management firms
    - Buying offices
    - Piggy-backing
    - Export houses
  - Direct
    - Wholesalers
    - Distributors
    - Stockists
    - Agents
    - to final user
    - via company branch offices
  - E-commerce and Internet
- Overseas production
  - Licensing Franchising
  - Contract manufacture
  - Joint venture Consortium Strategic alliance
  - Wholly owned overseas production
    - Acqusition
    - Organic growth

	Exporting	Overseas production
Key issues?	Exchange rates, protectionism	Political risk; partnership; managing overseas facilities; more risky
Involvement	Usually less involved, but an exporter might depend on the **overseas** market	Usually more involved, but overseas subsidiaries might act independently: varying levels of control and risk

The usual strategic tests of suitability, acceptability and feasibility apply to the selection of an entry method. A wide range of factors must be considered.

- **Company** size, experience and resources especially **finance**

- **Marketing objectives** for volume, timescale and market coverage

- **Mode availability** and quality in the target market

- **Human resource** requirements and availability of potential recruits

- **Marketing information** feedback available from potential methods of entry

- **Learning requirements** if expansion planned on a large scale

- Overseas production will generally be significantly more expensive

- **Control required:** any 3rd parties such as agents, distributors and contract manufacturers will have their own priorities, which will make control more difficult

- **Risk:** increasing control will require a higher financial commitment

- **Political factors** will be important: labour law; rules on ownership and transfer prices; tariffs; taxation; remittance of profits

6: Market entry methods

Exporting can be easy and cheap; it can start small; it does not dilute economies of scale

Indirect Exports

- **Export houses** may be principals or agents and may specialise in export credit: cheap but not under control.

- **Export management companies** provide a full export service for commission. Full market control retained but no experience gained.

- **Piggy backing** or **complementary exporting**: one producer sells another's goods as well as its own. Cheap and low risk.

- **Buying offices** of foreign governments and companies: cheap and low risk.

Direct Exports

- **To final user:** no intermediary costs – or benefits (experience, finance).

- **Branch offices:** provide a high degree of control and marketing information but require significant investment and management effort.

- **Agents** can have extensive market knowledge and experience: low cost and risk but commitment may be low also. Probably best for fairly low but steady turnover.

- **Wholesalers, distributors, stockists** all trade on their own account. May be difficult to control, but provide a simple route to increased sales.

Advantages

- Reduced **storage and transportation costs**
- **Overcomes barriers to trade**
- Production costs *may* be lower
- Economies of scale *may* be available

Licensing and franchising

- **Licensing** allows an overseas producer to make and sell goods in return for royalties

- **Franchises** involve greater commitment but provide greater control over the market offering

Partnerships

- **Joint ventures** are formal arrangements to share risks, costs and profits. They can lead to excellent local knowledge, good control and controlled investment

- **Consortiums** are similar but looser partnerships based on working relationships

- **Strategic alliances** are collaborations, often between competitors, to provide wider geographical coverage or market capability.

Contract manufacture gives great control over the marketing mix without incurring fixed costs.

Wholly owned overseas production

- Enjoy all the profits
- Make all the decisions
- Gain experience directly
- No communication problems
- Complete integration possible

BUT!

- Provide all the finance
- Take all the risk
- No one to consult
- Potential for political problems
- Cultural problems

Organic growth

- May be slow
- Minimises financial commitment
- Can be carefully controlled

Acquisition

- Fast route to brands and distribution
- Can provide good market knowledge
- Cultural complications in management

7: The marketing mix

This is a long chapter since the marketing mix is a large and well developed field. As well as the seven Ps, we also cover the closely related ideas of branding and relationship marketing.

The extended mix

Services are the most important sector of all developed economies so the **extended marketing mix** should be the basis of thinking.

- Product
- Price
- Promotion
- Place
- People
- Processes
- Physical evidence

Design issues for the marketing mix

Issue	Comment
Profit/volume	The mix can aim to maximise **sales** or **profits**. All other things being equal, the mix design should maximise profits.
Brand value	The mix should, where relevant, support brand values. Not all firms depend on branding.
Customers and distribution	The mix should satisfy customer needs: both the end-user and the intermediary or reseller.
Life cycle	The appropriate mix changes over the life cycle of the product. For example, a firm might adopt **penetration** or **skimming** prices at launch.
Marketing environment	The environment should be taken into account early in the planning process.
Seasonality	Clothes retailers are seasonally based, hence sales after Christmas.
Integration	The elements of the marketing mix must support each other.
Push/pull	The mix can pull demand through the distribution chain or push it down.
Competitive strategy	The mix will support the competitive strategy.

Product

A *product* is a package of benefits meeting particular needs. It is anything that can be offered to a market for attention, acquisition, use or consumption that might satisfy a want or need.

Product aspect

Physical: What it is (physical evidence)

Functional: What it does

Symbolic: What it says about the purchaser

Product levels

Core benefit: hotel offers rest and sleep away from home
Generic product: any hotel is a building with rooms to rent
Expected product: most expect cleanliness and quiet
Augmented product: additional benefits (eg swimming pool)
Potential product: possible augmentations in the future

Strategic issues

- Product definition: product is the starting point for differentiation to meet varying segment needs
- Product range: **width** (how many segments) and **depth** (how many options in each segment)
- Building the **brand**: quality, image, style, functionality
- Managing the **product portfolio** (Boston matrix, GE screen)
- **Quality**: fitness for use- depends on quality of both design and conformance

Price

Customers

- Generally, a lower price should increase quantity sold but inelastic demand may almost ignore price changes (eg petrol, tobacco, alcohol)
- Higher prices may lead to higher profits if improved quality sustains demand
- Distributors have their own priorities and profit targets
- Customers may notice fluctuations more than the general level of prices
- Customers may see pricing in ethical terms (eg medicines, 'windfall' profits)

The company

Suppliers must cover their costs if they are to survive. Price adjustments impact directly on profit.

Competitors

- There may be an industry **price leader**, whose price changes are generally followed by other firms
- **Commodities** generally trade at **market price**
- Price cuts may lead to **price war**: enhancement of some **aspect** of the product may be a better response
- Own-label brands are improving in quality: other brands must offer more

Place

Place or distribution includes both logistics (storage, transport) and channel (agents, wholesalers, stockists and so on)

- Trends in **logistics** include **JIT** and **out sourcing**.
- **Channel choice** involves a trade off between **cost** and **control**.
- **Direct sales** of several types (Internet, mail order, telephone order, TV shopping) are increasing.
- **Retailers** are gaining power over manufacturers as a result of their **purchasing power**, sales of their own brands and EFTPOS/loyalty card data gathering.
- Physical distributions' share of **total cost** is rising.
- **Just in Time** requires frequent small deliveries.

Promotion

Promotion is the element of the mix most under the control of the marketing department

Marketing communications should be **integrated** with overall strategy and within the range of communication methods

Forms of promotion

Each form must be managed in terms of

Advertising

Sales promotion

Personal selling

Public relations

Role – the target audience

Objectives – should be specific

Processes – such as purchasing, recruitment

Interpretation – each form with the others

Key strategic developments in promotion

Database marketing and data mixing   Highly targeted messages

Multiplicity of TV channels   Difficult to reach a large audience, easy to reach a specific one

Call centres   Can be the most important point of contact

Internet advertising   Becoming much more targeted

Political lobbying   Increasing national and supa-national regulation (eg EU, WTO) requires early influence

Characteristics of services

- **Intangibility** – no physical existence
- **Inseparability** – consumed as created
- **Perishability** – cannot be stored
- **Variability** – depends on individuals

All this leads to the marketing of an **attractive image**, which in turn leads to an emphasis on achieving a high quality of service provision

People

People are crucial to the provisional good service, particularly front-line workers. Managers must attend to motivation, job design and corporate culture.

Processes

Service is delivered on internal **processes**: the quality of the one depends on the effectiveness of the other.

Physical evidence

Physical evidence can overcome some of the intangibility. Aspects are the **environment** or ambience of the service, the **facilities** used and the **tangible evidence** the customer is left with (eg tickets, brochures).

7: The marketing mix

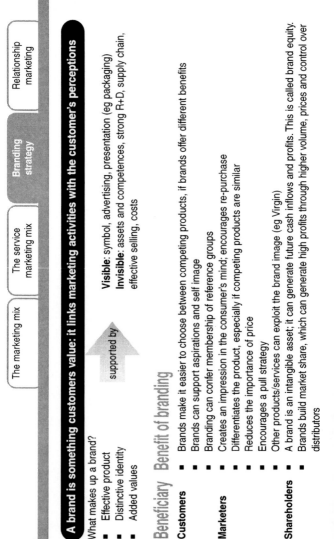

A brand is something customers value: it links marketing activities with the customer's perceptions

What makes up a brand?

- Effective product
- Distinctive identity
- Added values

supported by

Visible: symbol, advertising, presentation (eg packaging)

Invisible: assets and competences, strong R+D, supply chain, effective selling, costs

Beneficiary | Benefit of branding

Customers
- Brands make it easier to choose between competing products, if brands offer different benefits
- Brands can support aspirations and self image
- Branding can confer membership of reference groups

Marketers
- Creates an impression in the consumer's mind; encourages re-purchase
- Differentiates the product, especially if competing products are similar
- Reduces the importance of price
- Encourages a pull strategy
- Other products/services can exploit the brand image (eg Virgin)

Shareholders
- A brand is an intangible asset; it can generate future cash inflows and profits. This is called brand equity.
- Brands build market share, which can generate high profits through higher volume, prices and control over distributors

Brand values (brand image)

The added value conferred by a brand exists largely in the customer's mind. Buying decisions need not depend on product functionality: products may be bought for emotional reasons; also, branding reduces the need for judgement.

Brand values (or image) are built by:

- **Experience** of using the products
- **User associations**: particularly peer and aspiration groups and celebrities
- **Appearance**: aesthetic sensibility

Building brands

1 Product of appropriate quality

2 Build the basic brand to deliver the core product in an attractive way

3 Augment the product

4 Use the mix to build brand loyalty

5 Know where to stop

Revitalising brands

Increase sales volume by expanding into new markets and segments, funding new uses for existing products and developing new products (cf Ansoff matrix)

Brand extension is the use of a brand name established in one market to enter another. It is called *brand stretching* if the markets are very different.

Existing core values must be relevant to the new market. Conversely, the new market operation must not jeopardise the brand (eg by inappropriate associations).

Extending a brand is cheaper and less risky than building a new one, and encourages trial by the customer.

However, the brand needs substantial existing strength and the mix must generate some competitive advantage. Excessive extension can dilute brand values.

Brands in the global market place

- A **global brand** can offer a largely standardised product and use a common approach to the marketing mix

- A brand name may not be available for legal reasons **in a given country**

- Global brands attract imitators and counterfeiters

- Global brand names may have inappropriate connotations in some languages

- A **local brand** can reflect local needs and preferences

- Secondary brands are often local brands

- The expense of promoting a global brand may not be worthwhile in some markets (eg very price sensitive ones)

- Local brands may be more suited to local pronunciation and spelling

Relationship marketing

In commodity markets, price is the main concern and there is always a chance of a sale. Where products are differentiated, the aim should be a long-term relationship.

Implementing B2B relationship marketing

1 Identify key customers

2 Assign relationship managers

3 Develop clear job descriptions

4 Supervise the relationship managers

5 Develop long-term relationship plans

The importance of customer care

- Product liability legislation
- Industry codes of conduct
- Potential for market feedback
- Opportunity for differentiation
- Repeat purchases cost less in terms of promotion and overhead costs than converting non-buyers
- Even mildly dissatisfied customers are likely to go elsewhere rather than to complain

Relationship marketing seeks to enhance satisfaction by precision in meeting the needs of individual customers.

1 Build a customer database. IT has huge potential. Customers' records can be integrated with customer service phone systems. Customer preferences can be used to develop new products and simplify sales procedures.

2 Develop customer-oriented service systems. Improve on customer care to impress the customer and extend the relationship beyond the initial transaction. Culture, recruitment, training, technology and processes must be right and work well.

3 Promote extra direct contacts with customers. Each contact is an opportunity to promote the relationship and to obtain feedback.

Notes

8: The global product portfolio

This chapter is concerned with the strategic management of the product component of the marketing mix in the global context.

Strategic implications of the product life cycle

	PHASE			
	Introduction	Growth	Maturity	Decline
Product	Quality variable Product design and development vital Frequent design changes	Competitor's products have marked quality and technical differences Quality improves Product reliability may be important	Products become more standardised and differences between competing products less distinct	Products even less differentiated Quality becomes more variable
Customers	Initial customers willing to pay high prices Customers need to be convinced about buying	Customers increase in number	Mass market Market saturation Repeat-buying Markets become segmented	Customers are sophisticated buyers of a product they understand well
Marketing issues	High advertising and sales promotion costs High prices possible Distribution problematic	High advertising costs still, but as a % of sales, costs are falling Prices falling More distributors	Segment specific Choose best distribution Brand image	Less money spent on advertising and sales promotion

PHASE				
	Introduction	Growth	Maturity	Decline
Competition	Few or no competitors	More competitors enter the market Barriers to entry can be important	Competition at its keenest: on prices, branding, servicing customers, packaging etc	Competitors gradually exit from the market Exit barriers can be important
Profit margins	High prices but losses due to high fixed costs	High prices. High contribution margins, and increasing profit margins	Falling prices but good profit from high sales volume High prices in some market segments	Still low prices but falling profits as sales volume falls. Increases in prices may occur in the late decline stage
Manufacturing and distribution	Overcapacity High production costs Few distribution channels High labour skill content in manufacture	Undercapacity Move towards mass production and less reliance on skilled labour Distribution channels vital to marketing success	Optimum capacity Low labour skills Distribution channels fully developed, but less successful channels might be cut	Overcapacity because mass production techniques still used Distribution channels dwindling

8: The global product portfolio

Classification of goods

Consumer goods

- Convenience goods (eg groceries)
- Shopping on durable goods (eg a TV)
- Speciality goods (eg jewellry)
- Unsought goods

Industrial goods

- Installations (eg plant and machinery)
- Accessories (eg a printer for a PC)
- Raw materials
- Components
- Supplies (eg stationery, janitorial)

Applying the PLC

- It is difficult to define the boundaries of the stages and therefore to recognise them.

- The normal succession of the stages is not always evident.

- Stages can be extended or rearranged by marketing action such as promotion or re-positioning.

- Strategic implications of the PLC vary from industry to industry according to the nature of competition.

The product portfolio must be managed to ensure balance in terms of present and future cash flows, profits, growth and decline.

The BCG Matrix

		Star	Question mark
Market growth	High	Cash cow	Dog
	Low	High	Low

Market share relative to largest competitor

Stars – build
Cash cows – hold or harvest
Question marks – hold or harvest
Dogs – divest or hold

	Strong	Invest for growth	Invest selectively for growth	Develop for income
Company strength	Average	Invest selectively and build	Develop selectively for income	Harvest or divest
	Weak	Develop selectively Build on Strengths	Harvest	Divest
		Attractive	Average	Unattractive

Industry attractiveness

8: The global product portfolio

The same product may experience different life cycles in different national markets, depending on local conditions and marketing decisions taken.

- Typically, a product will be developed and launched in a single country. Launch in other countries will depend on factors such as market potential, possibility of launch by competitors and production volume.

- In highly competitive industries such as mobile phones and cameras, new products will be launched almost simultaneously in many markets and will experience very similarly phased life cycles.

Where the more traditional diffusion process occurs, the product may well follow this cycle:

1 Developed in a high income country and made there

2 Foreign production started by competitors

3 Foreign producers compete with originator in global markets

4 Foreign producers compete with originator in its home market

Standardisation of product and promotion across global markets can reap huge economies of scale; adaptation to local needs and wants can markedly increase sales.

Factors encouraging product standardisation

- Economies of scale
- Ease of management
- Homegenous markets
- Lack of cultural impact
- Consumer mobility
- Prestige brands and origins
- Low proportion of output for export

Factors encouraging product adaptation

- Legal requirements such as safety aspects
- Technical standards
- Market characteristics
- Education standards
  - Disposable income
  - Maintenance and repair facilities
  - Cultural impact

8: The global product portfolio

Attitudes to international marketing

Ethnocentrism: the home market dominates strategy; little adoption if any mix element; export often seen as a way to dispose of surpluses.

Polycentrism: strategy is decentralised to local operating companies; little co-ordination or standardisation, adoption at its most extreme.

Geocentrism: strategy is global with standardisation where possible and adaptation where necessary.

Marketing communications

Communications

Product	Standard	Adapted
Standard	Used by occasional exporters and for some global products, eg Pepsi Cola	Used where the same product meets different needs in different countries
Adapt	Used where a product meets the same need in several markets but conditions of use vary	Costly approach – may be required for full potential of a market to be developed

Encouraging innovation

1 **Imagining:** the initial insight into a market or a technology

2 **Incubating** the idea to see if it can be commercialised

3 **Demonstrating** prototypes to potential customers and obtaining feedback

4 **Promoting:** persuading the market to accept the innovation

5 Ensuring the outcome has as long a life as possible.

Steps 1–3 depend on the existence of a culture of innovation and learning.

Opportunities for innovation

- Exploiting unexpected success
- Exploring and explaining the reasons why what was supposed to happen didn't
- Overcoming inadequacies in underlying processes
- Exploiting changes in industry or market structure
- Demographic changes
- Changes in fashion
- Exploiting new knowledge and new technology

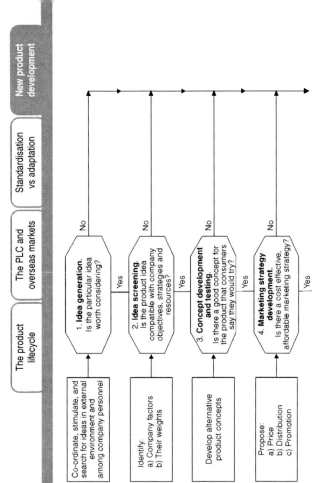

Co-ordinate, stimulate, and search for ideas in external environment and among company personnel

→ **1. Idea generation.** Is the particular idea worth considering? — No →
Yes ↓

Identify:
a) Company factors
b) Their weights

→ **2. Idea screening.** Is the product idea compatible with company objectives, strategies and resources? — No →
Yes ↓

Develop alternative product concepts

→ **3. Concept development and testing.** Is there a good concept for the product that consumers say they would try? — No →
Yes ↓

Propose:
a) Price
b) Distribution
c) Promotion

→ **4. Marketing strategy development.** Is there a cost effective, affordable marketing strategy? — No →
Yes ↓

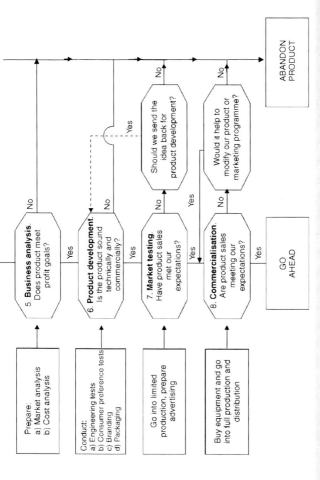

8: The global product portfolio

A *learning organisation* puts training and development at the heart of its strategy. It seeks to enhance both its strategic capability and its operations at all levels by continually expanding and utilising knowledge of all kinds. An important aspect is an emphasis on learning by staff at all levels.

Senge suggests 5 essential aspects to the development of the learning organisation.

- **Building a shared vision** focuses everybody's efforts around a single purpose.
- **Personal mastery** by workers at all levels, enhancing their own competence.
- **Mental models** are people's fundamental assumptions about how things should be done. It is necessary that these assumptions be challenged since they hamper fundamental developments.
- **Team learning** must be applied to problems by teams: individual learning is insufficient. Knowledge must be transferred and utilised not hoarded.
- **Systems thinking** tackles problems as wholes rather than breaking them down.

Implications of the learning approach

- Significant innovation can originate anywhere in the organisation.
- Organisation structures must respond to opportunities and changed conditions.
- Management must create a learning climate and create systems to apply knowledge to problems at all levels.

9: Price and place

This chapter combines disussion of price and place. Price is a very complex topic: it is directly linked to revenue and so is very important, but it is also subject to many complex and often conflicting ideas and theories. It requires both knowledge and experience to administer effectively.

Place is equally complex, but much more practical to manage.

Topic List

Price

Pricing policy

Cost accounting and breakeven analysis

Place

Basic economics of pricing

- ## Perfect competition

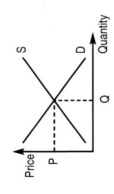

The price mechanism brings supply and demand together at the equilibrium price P. This is also the market clearing price since quantity Q is both offered and demanded and there is neither surplus nor shortage.

- **Monopolists** prevent other suppliers from entering the market and control the market price to make high profits.

- In **oligopoly**, a small group of suppliers control supply. They rarely compete on price, since a price cut by one woud be matched by others and all would lose profit without gaining market share.

- In **monopolistic competition**, suppliers pursue monopoly profit by **product differentiation**: the customer must be persuaded that the product is unique.

Price elasticity of demand (PED)

A measure of the change in **demand** for a good in response to a change in its **price**: when demand is **elastic** a small change in price produces a large change in demand. When the demand is inelastic, a large change in price produces only a small change in demand.

$$PED = \frac{\text{change in quantity demanded as \% of demand}}{\text{change in price as \% of price}} = \frac{\Delta Q}{Q} \times \frac{P}{\Delta P} = \frac{\Delta Q}{\Delta P}$$

P and Q may be values at a **point** or averages over an **arc**.

PED > 1 means that demand is **elastic.** An increase in price from P_A to P_B leads to a fall in total expenditure:

Area Y is greater than area X.

Price

P_B
P_A

X
Y

D

Quantity

PED < 1 means that demand is **inelastic.** An increase in price from P_A to P_B leads to a rise in total expenditure:

Area X is greater than area Y.

Price

P_B
P_A

X
Y

D

Quantity

Notice that elasticity varies along a straight line demand curve!

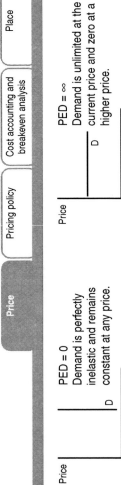

Price — Pricing policy — Cost accounting and breakeven analysis — Place

PED = 0
Demand is perfectly inelastic and remains constant at any price.

Price
D
Quantity

PED = ∞
Demand is unlimited at the current price and zero at a higher price.

Price
D
Quantity

When PED = 1, demand responds **proportionally** to any change in price and total expenditure is constant, whatever the price.

PED is affected by

Availability of substitutes

The most important influence. Easy availability of substitutes makes demand more elastic: price rises lead to substitution.

Time horizon

Elasticity is low in the short term. Over the longer term **provision** of substitutes and awareness of them increases.

Competitors' pricing

If competitors match price changes, each one will face inelastic demand. If some increase prices and others do not, the former will face elastic demand. Unmatched price cuts have a similar effect.

Influences on price setting

- **Costs**. Cost plus is a very simple approach and tends to ensure that profits are made. Retailers use a simple **mark up**. If cost is the only criterion, marketing opportunities may well be missed, since no attention is paid to demand.

- **Competition**. Oligopoly leads to **going rate** pricing, possibly determined by a price leader (which may not be the market leader). Matching another firm's price is not illegal unless there is actual **collusion**. There may be standard price differences between brands.

- **Demand**. The basic market clearing price approach can be modified by price discrimination between segments with different PED. Segmentation by location and product version is common; the most usual kind of price discrimination is by **time**, with higher charges at peak periods.

Pricing policy

Price sensitivity

Those who spend other people's money (eg in B2B) are less price sensitive. Other factors:

- Concept of a 'fair price'
- One off purchases involve price comparisons.
- 'Bargain price' overcomes caution.
- With HP and leasing, cashflow is more important than total price.
- When prices rise, perceived value lags behind.

Influences on price decisions

- Intermediaries' profit objectives
- Competitors' actions
- Supplier awareness of purchasers' rising revenues
- Inflation
- Quality connotations
- Reference prices for new products
- Levels of disposable income
- Product range eg loss leaders, high prices for spares
- Public reaction to shortages of commodities

Pricing strategies

- Market penetration
- Market skimming
- Early cash recovery
- Product line promotion
- Distributor autonomy
- Cost plus
- Target pricing
- Pricing discrimination
- Going rate
- Quantum (price point)
- Odd number
- One coin purchase
- Gift purchase price points

Direct costs (variable costs, marginal costs) vary directly with the volume of output

Overhead costs arise whether production takes place or not

Absorption costing calculates product cost including overheads

- Legal requirement for stock valuation in published accounts
- Basis of cost plus pricing

Direct costs are more appropriate to short term decisions such as pricing

Contribution is sales value minus variable costs of sale. C/S ratio = $\dfrac{\text{contribution}}{\text{selling price}}$

Breakeven volume of sales occurs when contribution covers fixed costs

$\Rightarrow$ Sales volume required to breakeven = $\dfrac{\text{Total fixed costs}}{\text{Contribution per unit}}$

...and sales revenue required to breakeven = $\dfrac{\text{Total fixed costs}}{\text{C/S ratio}}$

Margin of safety = excess of sales over breakeven point

Direct distribution

No intermediaries used. May be based on media (eg direct mail) or own sales force.

- Use if intermediaries unwilling, uncooperative or tied to competitors
- Easy if competitors are concentrated geographically
- Expert sales force needed
- Fits well with use of specialised transport or distribution equipment

Indirect distribution

Intermediaries are used

- May be cheaper and easier than training, managing and paying own sales force
- May require less marketing effort and skill
- Narrow range may fit well into distributor's wider range
- Sales in bulk require less administrative effort
- Distributors can give wide geographic coverage

Distribution functions

- Transport
- Stock holding and storage
- Local market knowledge
- Local promotion
- Display

Channel design influences

- Customer habits and needs
- Product characteristics
- Distributor characteristics
- Competitor channel choices
- Supplier characteristics

Channel dynamics and vertical marketing systems

Disputes between players in indirect channels can be minimised and resolved by vertical marketing system relationships. These aim to integrate the members in joint problem solving and the pursuit of common objectives.

- Corporate systems are integrated under single ownership

- Contractual systems have extensive legal relationships (eg franchising)

- Administrative systems are based on agreement on standards and systems

Supply chain developments

Major global manufacturers are cutting costs by adopting JIT logistics and integrating their supply chains more closely.

- Lead times are compressed

- Freedom of action is reduced

- Competition is now between complete supply chains rather than between manufacturers or between distributors

- The chain becomes a network rather than a pipeline, optimising the activities of companies working together to support customers

10: Ethical considerations

Ethics is a very hot topic in business because of recent gross failures such as Enron and Parmalat. Ethics should be incorporated into the strategy of the organisation and be a guide to its implementation.

Corporate social responsibility is a separate (though linked) topic that can usefully be approached with ethical ideas in mind.

Ethics is about right and wrong and how conduct should be judged to good or bad. It exists independently of religious faith and legal rules. Non-cognitivism suggest that all moral statements are merely subjective and that ideas of right and wrong may vary, particularly between cultures. Cognitivist approaches propose that objective, universally applicable moral truths exist and can be known.

- The **consequentialist** approach judges actions by their consequences. This leads to **utilitarianism** and the moral desirability of the greatest good for the greatest number of people.

- Virtue ethics is based on the cultivation of suitable virtues to guide behaviour, such as fairness, honesty, determination and empathy.

- The **deontological** approach judges actions by reference to **categorical imperatives**. *Kant* proposed two important rules:

  1 Never act in a way you would condemn in others

  2 Do not treat people simply as a means to an end

- **Natural law** approaches are today concerned with 'human rights' and the duty to respect them.

Social responsibility of business is ill-defined in common usage but focuses on the provision of specific benefits to society beyond the scope of the organisation's commercial purpose. Examples include charitable donations, the preservation of employment and spending on environmental purposes.

Arguments for

- Many groups have a stake in what the organisation does; and the law does not adequately protect those affected by business actions

- Business cannot exist without inputs from society such as economic infrastructure

- Capitalism is inherently exploitative and inequitable

- Shareholders are generally ineffective at controlling management

Arguments against

- Legal respect for property rights mean that shareholders' ownership must not be abused

- Businesses benefit society by their economic activity: output and employment result

- Improper activity should be the business of law-makers not unrepresentative pressure groups

- Most large businesses are owned by institutional investors such as pension funds and insurance companies that provide widely available social benefits

Ethical stance

The extent to which an organisation will exceed its minimum obligation to stakeholders. *(Johnson & Scholes)*

- **Short term stakeholder interest:** obey the letter of the law

- **Long term stakeholder interest:** behave ethically to enhance image and reduce pressure for regulation

- **Multiple stakeholder obligations:** the expectations of other groups of stakeholders may be considered, as well as any right they may have

- **Shaper of society:** really restricted to public sector organisations; businesses should not sacrifice their commercial viability

Ethical dilemmas

Conflicting views of the organisation's responsibilities create ethical dilemmas for managers at all levels.

- Dealing with corrupt or unpleasant regimes
- Honesty in advertising
- Employees – cost or asset?
- Corrupt payments to officials – extortion, bribery or gift? The local culture must be considered.

The conduct of a organisation's senior officers constitutes its **corporate governance**. The influence of those officers over the behaviour of the organisation and the potential for both PR and financial disaster make this a matter of strategic importance.

External measures to improve corporate governance

1 **Accounting standards** attempt to inhibit financial manipulation.

2 **Codes of professional conduct** regulate many senior managers.

3 **Commissions on standards of behaviour** (in the UK) have established best practice.

Free flow of information

to stakeholders tends to inhibit wrong doing by senior managers. However, commercial confidentiality must be respected.

Structural measures

Non-executive directors

may remain objective and ensure proper governance in such areas as ethics, audit and senior manager remuneration. However, there are now accusations of partiality within a close-knit body of non-executives in the UK.

Two approaches to managing ethics

Compliance-based

Aim: to ensure that the organisation acts within the law.

- Compliance procedures
- Internal audit
- Disciplinary procedures
- Protection for whistle blowers

Integrity-based

Aim: to promote the proper excercise of managerial responsibility

- Establish ethical standards
- Leadership from the very top
- Integrate standards into culture
- Create sense of shared accountability

The *societal marketing concept* (Kotler): doing business in a way that preserves or enhances the customer's and society's well-being

Ethics and the marketing mix

- **Product**

  Risks of use (eg tobacco)

  Quality expectations

  Environmental impact of industry

- **Promotion**

  Advertising honest, decent, legal?

  Promotion to children

- **Price**

  Price fixing by cartels

  Deceptive or opaque pricing that misleads about the total costing

- **Place**

  Exploitation of intermediaries (eg delaying due payments)

Notes